T0355009

# RISE
# BEYOND
# LIMITS

# RISE BEYOND LIMITS:

## A
## Blueprint
## for
## Success

## MICHAEL BRITT

This book is a work of non-fiction. Unless otherwise noted, the author
and the publisher make no explicit guarantees as to the accuracy of
the information contained in this book and in some cases, names of
people and places have been altered to protect their privacy.

Archway Publishing books may be ordered through booksellers or by contacting:

Archway Publishing
1663 Liberty Drive
Bloomington, IN 47403
www.archwaypublishing.com
844-669-3957

Because of the dynamic nature of the Internet, any web addresses or
links contained in this book may have changed since publication and
may no longer be valid. The views expressed in this work are solely those
of the author and do not necessarily reflect the views of the publisher,
and the publisher hereby disclaims any responsibility for them.

Any people depicted in stock imagery provided by Getty Images are
models, and such images are being used for illustrative purposes only.
Certain stock imagery © Getty Images.

ISBN: 978-1-6657-6269-4 (sc)
ISBN: 978-1-6657-6271-7 (hc)
ISBN: 978-1-6657-6270-0 (e)

Library of Congress Control Number: 2024913700

Print information available on the last page.

Archway Publishing rev. date: 11/04/2024

# CONTENTS

# INTRODUCTION

In the past, and quite recently, I've been approached by individuals and representatives connected to some of the largest and most popular media organizations in the country. This is because I have been able to produce such an impressive list of accomplishments in such a brief time. I started walking this journey as young Black male in America who knows exactly what it feels like to come from humble beginnings. The manifested results have been nothing short of astonishing.

It's no surprise that these various media outlets crave the details of how I happened to not only beat the odds but continue to prevail. The short answer for this is simple and can only be described as divine destiny. Of course, this all started with me imagining a great life for myself and those who depend on me. But one never truly knows if their visualizations will cause God to laugh or not. So just imagine cooking up the perfect plan, but you already had all the sauce to go with it.

It's a well-known fact that I've been involved in the negotiations of multi-million-dollar real estate deals and have also played a critical role in the struggle for change within the

Criminal Justice System in Virginia whether its moral progress, financial, or spiritual. For me, it all translates as success. These things and others are what fuel the allure of my lifestyle. Some call me Lil Mike, some address me as Mr. Absolutely but regardless of what name the world knows me by it will never mean anything if I'm not being me. I feel as if I was placed on this earth with just as much responsibility as I have blessings. It is imperative that I do everything within my power to spread knowledge and direction in hopes that it'll help others achieve their dreams.

I've come to the realization that there are a lot of people who look up to me. I thought most of them were younger, but this group includes more older people than I would have ever expected. Nevertheless, most of them can relate to one very vital commonality; They were never exposed to the facts, given adequate tools, or provided with the direction that true success demands.

Because of where I am today financially, spiritually, and emotionally don't be surprised if there was some tribulation or just a flat-out hard knock life. It would be a mistake for anyone to think that I did not have to fight, get knocked down, rise again, and then continue to get knocked down before I finally gained the proper footing needed to land some solid blows of my own.

So, after succeeding in a toe-to-toe battle against fear, worry, doubt and a lot of hate from various places, do not dare to ask me if I'm ready for whatever else the world might throw my way. Because there is only one answer to that, Abso-fucking-lutely! Over time I developed patience which allowed me to appreciate the small steps because before I knew it, they became giant leaps that landed me right on top of every goal I set.

Most of all this is why we must never forget that sometimes it's the little things that count. This is how one goes from the point of despair and "Duress" in the financial or even life situation to that place of "success" we all seek according to one's own definition.

So loved ones allow me to invite you in and provide you with a backstage pass and an behind the scenes look, not into some industry event, celebrity party, or Hollywood premiere but what this book seeks to offer is an exclusive glimpse into the use of techniques and the creation of a mentality necessary to prepare your mind, body, and spirit to become the platform to receive the greatness you were destined to achieve.

WELCOME TO THE V.I.P SECTION! Do I mean that literally? ABSOFUCKNGLUTELY!!! This book is going to introduce you to the reality of this "great" country we live in, and the thought process and attitude you will need to develop or sharpen to succeed, not only here but anywhere life takes you. The following chapters will provide you with a glimpse of my experiences accompanied with valid information to guide you on your quest to greatness. So, when you read anything under the title "V.I.P Section" take it seriously. Enjoy!

*"What you did before had an effect on
what's happening now but what you do
now will effect what happens later."*
—Michael Britt

CHAPTER 1

# THE AMERICAN DREAM: WHAT?

THE IDEALISTIC DEFINITION OF THE AMERICAN DREAM can be identified as the supreme standard of freedom, happiness, and the opportunity of success without boundaries. A concept advertised to the world in such a way that it's sought after by individuals from every corner of the world. How many people do you think have risked life and limb to turn their fantasy into reality? And this question doesn't only apply to those who are native to this country either. For example, the hundreds of thousands of immigrants who take the treacherous routes from Mexico or South America just to get here. For all that they endure—sickness, risk of prosecution, and even death—it could be said that they consider America as there land of milk and honey. But the concept of how great the opportunity is in this country remains paradox. This is supported by so many people's dreams that have already turned out to be nightmares.

The American dream is defined as "the belief that anyone, regardless of where they were born or what class they were born into, can attain their own version of success in which upward mobility is possible for everyone."

Unfortunately, this concept seems to ignore a fact of America's reality. Sacrifice, hard work, and even a good balance of risk taking should be all that is required to get a person to their ultimate goal. It should never be based purely upon chance or some other factor that leaves a person with zero control.

Pull yourself up by the bootstraps, such a famous idiom used in our culture to inspire a person to get things done no matter what circumstance. But what about all those hidden factors that cause statements like that to seem almost irrelevant? I am talking about the full history of slavery, systemic racism, poverty, social economics, etc. I recommend that you read the book *Post Traumatic Slave Syndrome (American Legacy of Enduring Injury & Healing)* by Dr. Joy Degroy.

Just to give you a quick history lesson, the term "American Dream" was coined by author James Truslow Adams in his 1931 bestselling book *Epic of America.* In it he describes it as that dream of a land in which life should be better, richer, and fuller for everyone according to ability or achievement. Ha! Say what? It does not take too much looking around to see that this obviously doesn't apply to everyone. The author went on to say, "It is a difficult dream for the European Upper-class to interpret adequately, and too many of us ourselves have grown weary and mistrustful of it. It is not a dream of motor cars and high wages, but a dream of social order in which each man and woman shall be able to attain the fullest stature of which they are innately capable, and be recognized by others for what they are, regardless of the fortuitous circumstances of birth or position."

RZA from Wu-Tang put me on game to a very serious understanding about this order: knowledge, wisdom/understanding, freedom, justice, equality, food, clothing, shelter, love, peace, and happiness. When a person possesses knowledge, wisdom, and understanding, the pursuit of freedom becomes possible. This freedom, however, must be grounded in the principles of justice. If someone deliberately harms you, justice must prevail to maintain equality. Any action disrupting this balance requires accountability. Basic necessities like food, clothing, and shelter are essential for personal well-being and peace. Beyond these, love is a fundamental entitlement, encompassing all the key elements mentioned.

What a cute sentiment, right? But how many open their eyes and wake up to the reality of a home surrounded by a white picket fence, located in a nice neighborhood full of happy children, and maybe a pet or two running across bright-green manicured lawns as married couples smile upon them? If you could hear me at this point in the book, I'd be making a record scratch sound that's in all the throwback movies when somebody hits pause. Then I'd play you the other version of this song. The one where the picket fence becomes a steel one that young black kids jump over as they run from the police through a neighborhood full of addicts of all types. No bright-green grass and no married couples who don't know what it feels like to be on welfare. These streets are full of single mothers pushing baby strollers to the bus stop to visit their father in jail. Maybe he lacked guidance, or maybe he couldn't fathom any other way to feed his child besides taking a penitentiary chance? Many black men make that choice for many different reasons. It just seems so much easier for them to make that choice when it's fueled by the pursuit of riches. And in this attempt to succeed at that goal is where a person becomes disconnected with others, themselves, and even the presence of a higher power above us all. This will, without a doubt, leave anybody with a feeling of uncertainty and lack of direction.

Careful not to make excuses for anyone who decides not to live out their life doing things the right way, I must never neglect to acknowledge that most of society is deeply rooted in a cycle of hand-to-mouth syndrome. The vast majority is living paycheck to paycheck, and these checks are often being spent before they even come in. You can almost compare it with insanity—the way that people with so little seem to have no issue with the inevitable consequences of living above their means. Past generations called it "Keeping up with the Jones,' but today it's more like Keeping up with the Kardashians."

Stand out and gain attention by any means has become the new status quo. Thus, the evolution of slavery is now a financial one, and this is what the American dream means for so many. It's to the point where there aren't too many people who look forward to waking up for work. And why would they when all they're working toward is the achievement of someone else's dream? I don't look down upon anyone who's all about hard work and just wants to keep a steady, easy job. But I also believe that people should have more options, with resources included, to pursue their bigger goals, rather than have little to no choice but to settle on whatever comes their way. For this reason, among others, I've asked myself what I can do. My answer has become this book. Within these pages I give you my advice, guidance, and knowledge of how to successfully apply specific techniques to even the odds in the fight for a better life.

My hope is that you read this book and believe in yourself enough to step into that greatness that exists in us all. If I can do it, anyone can. Just always remember to never limit yourself to fit someone else's definition of success. By the time you finish reading this book I will have explained every step you'll need to take to end up in the best financial position possible. In particular, I will be going in detail about how to not only clean up credit history but I will give you the game on how to build it as well.

Before I do that, though, allow me to share with you my philosophy pertaining to the state of mind you must be in and the spiritual awareness you should have before using any information provided in this book. After all, everything I'm able to give you is because I've always believed in a power greater than myself.

After a lot of long and deep thoughts, I've come to realize that the link that binds the spirit to the flesh is one that has never been accurately described with words. It has no shape or physical form that man is readily aware of. All one can say is that it is divine. You can call yourself a Christian, a Muslim, a Buddhist, or even a Scientologist. But even considering all the differences between the various factions, one thing that should never be a cause of conflict between them is the truth of there being only one infinite source of all we know and all we ever will know.

Say "God" in any language you want, and it still means the same thing. Do you really think you'll be the first or last to give a name or title to that which has no beginning or end? My point here is that as humans we put too much of our energy into what to say about rather than what to do about that something.

Regardless of what you believe in, who you may pray to, or which religious sector you are a part of, there is one common similarity that we all share. The bestowed blessing of divine energy and the ability to tap into that energy for the purpose of experiencing a peaceful, prosperous, loving, and fulfilling life. The ways of the world we live in today cause us to lose sight of this by being a consistent conduit for jealousy, envy, rage, worry, hate. The list goes on. Now let me ask you: what person, or people, in your life can cause you the highest degree of spiritual, mental, and physical pain by perpetuating these emotions? If your answer wasn't the person in the mirror, then you're completely wrong. One thing about this divine energy, paired with free will, is that it can be used in one way or the other. There is no in between when it comes to good or evil, love or hate, righteousness or unrighteousness. You have more power than anyone when it comes to building or destroying yourself. Ultimately, the choice is yours.

So, my advice to you is that you believe in who you are, step into your greatness, and turn your dreams into reality. So, what is it that you dream of? Maybe it's to buy a $100,000 car? Or having the deed to a seven-bedroom home? For sure, there are a lot of people whose goals is to simply live well while maintaining good health. None of these answers are wrong but they're not exactly right either. Your spirit should seek to be happy, content, and completely at peace as you make the journey toward what it is that you want out of life. So many have discovered that the destination means so much more if they're sure to acknowledge and appreciate what it took to get there. The longer you must run to get to where you're going is nothing but a testament to just how far you've made it. The harder you fall is the greater opportunity to discover exactly what you can get back up from.

So, three things you do before you start your journey: 1. Analyze what exactly it is that you want, what you're willing to give, sacrifice or lose to get it. 2. Develop a solid plan of action and prepare yourself to have patience or adjust when things don't go your way. 3. Make final decisions, one of the quickest ways to failure is being indecisive or changing your mind too often. It's imperative that you find balance between making your mind up, and your mind making you make stuff up. If you stay focused, I guarantee that you can find opportunity in places and things that most people would overlook.

I'm reminded of a time back when I was a pre-teen and there were a lot of my peers showing up to school with these cheap little $2 silicon bracelets. They came in an assortment of different colors, and each of these colors represented a type of sexual act from kissing to lap dances, to full blown intercourse. You would simply pop the bracelet of the person you liked, and then it was on and popping!

I was absolutely a major player in that game, but once I realized how much of a trend the bracelets were the hustler in me was awakened. I began buying them only to bring them to school and double up off what I paid. This hustle inadvertently opened the door to another. One day as I pull some from my pocket to sell to a classmate, a condom fell from my pocket. This condom was obviously for my personal use, but when one of the fellas asked if he could buy it from me, it was like a pandora's box had been opened. The moral to the story is that I made so much money that I attracted the attention of the school faculty, who in turn notified my mom of my little endeavor. She was more concerned with what her son was doing with condoms more than anything. Ironically, it was that same condom money that kept our water on during a tough time.

Seeing my mother cry over bills she couldn't pay gave me a feeling that I never want to feel again. And as proud as I was to be able to do something about it, she was prouder of me, and made that crystal clear when she said to me that I'd "be the one."

I give you this story in hopes that you find yourself somewhere in it. Anybody, from anywhere under any circumstances can be great. The pursuit can be ugly, and it can be beautiful, but the result will remain what you build it to be. Be gentle with yourself through it all. You WILL make mistakes, but you'll be greater because of them.

# CHAPTER 2

# SUCCESS? BY WHO'S DEFINITION?

---

*"Reputation is built in a moment; Character is built in a lifetime; success is a journey not a destination ..."*

---

SO WHERE DO YOU START TO BEGIN THIS JOURNEY? THAT is the question one must ask themselves. And to discern the starting point we must first define what success means to us. To be successful in anything, you must first live in that "thing." You must be saturated by it to the point of it overflowing, leaving its mark on, not only every aspect of your life, but also those that come into any part of your sphere that you've created. There's no way you can possibly hit your mark and stay there if you and those around you are in bad shape financially. So, here's where I give you valuable jewels.

You need to understand your credit score and how it affects you. This number will move up or down between 300-850 based off your handling of loans and Loc's (lines of credit). There are five factors the score will be based off:

- Payment History
- Amounts Owed
- Length of Credit History
- Types of credit Used.
- New Credit

Payment History and amounts owed will have the biggest impact on your score, but the other 3 categories are important as well. I'll do my best to explain this as simply as I can without omitting important facts.

You can have "Revolving credit" or "Installment credit." "Revolving" basically means you'll have specific maximum amount you can spend. You can either pay it all back at the due date or make small payments to roll the rest over to the next billing cycle. "Installment" is a little straighter lined. You have your amount, and you make payments until it's all paid off.

9 things to remember when dealing with credit are:

1. Pay with credit card balances strategically and on time.
2. Ask for higher limits after you've proven to be reliable.
3. Become an authorized user (have someone with good credit add you onto their credit)
4. Pay bills on time (I told you!)
5. Dispute credit report errors (we'll talk about this next)
6. Deal with collections accounts (you don't want to be sued)
7. Use a secure credit card.
8. Get credit for rent and utility payments.
9. Add to your credit mix (apply for different type of credit

Going out into the world to accomplish your intentions and goals defined success well. That in and of itself looks different to everyone. All though being rich is nice, that doesn't necessarily completely define success. A person who's not rich but has enough to be in position to do what they want, when they want, has indeed achieved a level of success.

The recognition you receive from those who know you best is yet another level of success. You can be famous at home and be the King, Queen, Prince, or Princess of your castle. Being there to build foundational family structure does indeed define an important form of success in that area. Family, happiness, and time well spent indicates success.

You must also practice discipline, have resilience and supreme confidence in conjunction with never forgetting the importance of teamwork. Never allow the possibility of failure to prevent the attempt to strive for the goal of success. There are lessons in failure that can be life changing. At times, things may seem to be going wrong, when they're going right. Gain the ability to be strong even when everything is looking worse.

Furthermore, you must liberate yourself from that crab in a barrel mentality. You do not have to pull someone else down to come up. This mentality is counterproductive, and it is an antithesis to what success is and how to manifest it in your life. There does exist a way for us to all benefit and win. You must also remember that this, and certain "divide and conquer" strategies that we easily execute and propagate against one another were intentionally introduced into "certain communities in America as a calculated technique of control. Pick up a history book and train your mind to be ready for these vicious tactics. Einstein said it best: "Failing to prepare, is actually preparing to fail." Proper-planning-prevents-poor-performance. Remember these 5 P's as a tool to keep yourself grounded.

You should also stay aware and look for physical examples of success as well as the people they're attached to. This is one of the success manifestation principles I live by. People, places, and things along with what you put into your pursuit, will always have an influence on what the outcome will be.

Think hard about the moves you make, but even more, don't just think. Take action! "Thought without action is only a daydream and action without thought will eventually become a nightmare."

# V.I.P TAKEAWAYS

_____

_____

_____

_____

_____

_____

_____

_____

_____

_____

# CHAPTER 3

# THERE'S NO TIME TO PLAY

ONE OF THE MOST POWERFUL MESSAGES I'VE EVER HEARD come from brother, Joel Osteen, in his message titled, "Redeem the Time" he talks about how important it is that we remain focused on properly utilizing our time here on earth. I suggest that you check out this video and experience for yourself how powerful the message is.

It should be easy for you to realize that your most valuable commodity, more valuable than money, is time. Do not allow distractions or circumstances to keep you from making the most of your time. Allow me to remind you that you are a person of destiny. You have more than enough power to make a difference in this world and fulfill your purpose. You vigilantly shake off feelings of self-pity or disappointment. Keep your actions, thought, and complete attention focused on your goals.

Be careful not to dwell on the past, even looking too far into the future could be detrimental, so just do your best to stay in the moment.

I've come to realize that time is the only difference between me and a billionaire. That and a little opportunity. Maybe you feel like you're in too rough of a financial position to even think about pursuing an avenue to that kind of extreme wealth. So, here is where I provide you with a little push in the right direction.

These steps will explain the process of how to remove derogatory marks from your credit.

Step 1:

- Create a profile for Experian.com and CreditKarma.com

Step 2:

- On Experian.com look at everything that's on your report, what's negative and personal information you want removed.

Step 3:

- File dispute against anything you choose on your report.

Step 4:

- "Upload Document" Here you will be asked to take a front and back photo of your I.D. and screenshot your bank contact.

Step 5:

- Click "Inquires" and "File dispute"

Step 6:

- In the comments section you'll say:
  "15 US 1681 a4 states that I have the right to privacy.
  15 USC section 604 section 2 states that a consumer
  reporting agency cannot furnish an account without
  my written instructions."
  Within 24 to 72 hours, they will remove the personal
  into you disputed. It'll take about 15 to 30 days for the
  other stuff. If they decline the first time, get 609 letter
  that deals with debt verification and try again.

Once you feel that you have some room to breathe it should be easier to develop your plan of action. But you must approach this with what the world now calls, "The Mamba Mentality" (Rest in Power Kobe Bryant).

Chase after your dreams without fear and maximize your full potential. Supreme confidence in how you move is key. People as successful as Elon Musk, or a Jay-z always have this in common. Of course, they faced challenges and endured setbacks. But resilience is what allowed them to push through and learning from mistakes is what aided their survival. Nevertheless, it would be a mistake to think that any one person just becomes successful and stays that way all on their own.

Teamwork is pivotal, so be sure to surround yourself with

those who will be an asset to you on your journey. You'll need to assess strengths and weaknesses so that you are able to decide who belongs where within the ranks. Never allow your team to see you sweat. It's up to you to lead by example and set the tone for success. They should always look to you and see a loyal, responsible, and trustworthy person.

People admire someone who shows patience and discipline. "The thing man seeks is seeking him." That is a quote from Florence Scovel Shinn.

Your spirit should always guide you, not your emotions. Everything that is meant for you will come if you just put out the energy that it demands. Your thoughts and intentions have the power to draw good or bad things your way. If you think about events in your own life, good or bad, and can recall the state of mind you were in when they happened, you'll see that this is a fact.

A vision board can be another way to change your power of focus and attract the things you desire. Being able to see that car, or house, or healthy body will help you to recognize, as soon as you wake up, what opportunities are present, or approaching for you to move that much closer to your goal.

Along with watching how you think, you should watch how you speak. The tongue is powerful, and if you've ever heard anyone say, "speak it into existence," I surely hope you learned not to take those words lightly. Let your voice carry good and prosperity into the world. Verbalize your intentions and think "BIG" when you do it. There are no limits. If the plan is to have a million, speak to one-hundred million. That way if you fall short you still get what you wanted and maybe more.

I'll end this chapter by leaving you with a basic model summarizing the path of manifestation:

Watch your thoughts.
They become words.
Watch your words.
They become actions.
Watch your actions.
They become habits.
Watch your habits.
They become characters.
Watch your character.
It becomes your destiny …

# CHAPTER 4

# GIVE YOURSELF SOME CREDIT

EVERY NOW AND AGAIN IT IS OKAY TO GIVE YOURSELF A pat on the back. If you are doing everything that you should be, take time to be proud of yourself. Maybe even pop a bottle or take a trip somewhere to celebrate. Just go ahead and give yourself some credit, figuratively and literally!

In today's world credit is an important tool that you need to understand in order to navigate our country's financial system. This is such an important fact that I am going to go ahead and jump right into giving you the game.

Let's say you received a loan and have fully repaid the debt. Your credit report will now show what is called a tradeline.

These are one of the things that will help boost your credit score. Below is a process that can create these same trade-lines between you and a friend, family member or business entity.

- Draft, download or purchase sample promissory note from staples.
- Outline terms of agreement, types of collateral, loan amount, payment schedule, etc. (include serial #'s and VIN #'s of all items)
- Have local notaries notarized promissory note with a witness signature?
- File promissory note with the local county register's office to have it documented with a reg number.
- The secured party (loaner) files a UCC-1 with the promissory note. Give details of collateral being used.
- File UCC-3 for release of collateral as loan is paid off.

So, once you have a strong credit score you will have gained the ability to secure funding for a home, auto, new business, etc. Credit will be your tool to make big purchases. The banks will be able to trust you with loans because your credit report will show the history of settling your debts.

I would also recommend that you use personal credit

builders such as SELF, CREDIT STRONG, AVA, KICKOFF, EXTRA. The list goes on, so do your research to learn about other methods to boost your score. These companies charge a small fee to boost your credit score anywhere from 20 to 50 points.

Now, look at how credit scoring works. 35% is based on your payment history. So, pay your bills on time. 30% is derived from the amount owed. Having too much debt or taking more than you can afford can affect your score negatively. 15% is from your length of credit history. The longer you wisely use credit the better your score. 10% is based on new credit. Positive effects of this are from taking new credit sparingly and on time payment. Then they look at the type of credit profile.

To get the best interest rates and the highest chance of being approved for new lines of credit you'll want to maintain at least a 670 or above. 330-579 is very poor. 580-669 is fair. 670-739 is considered good. 740-799 can be very good. Very excellent, now that's between 800-850. Shoot for that baby.

Remember this when it comes to credit is not extra paper to play with. Use It for necessities only. If you "want" to buy something and you "don't" have the money, do not use your credit card instead. Charge no more than 20-30% of the limit at any one time. Pay the balance off every month if you want to avoid paying interest. If you pay on time, you will avoid late fees. Past due payments drop your score! Stay away from that baby!

Tell me something ... What? "We got da keys ... keys ... keys ... keys ... and that is what I got. So here, take these and open the financial doors to your future.

Pay Bills Strategically The portion of your credit limits that you're using at any time is called your credit utilization. Do not use more than 30%. Lower is better. People with the highest credit scores use less than 7%. Your credit utilization is the $2^{nd}$ biggest factor in your credit score.

Request Higher Credit Limits. When your limit goes up and your balances stay the same, it instantly lowers your credit utilization. That's a credit boost baby. An increase in income + years of positive credit use = a higher chance of limit increase.

Become an authorized User. If you have a friend or relative with a high credit limit on their card with a good history of on time payments, ask to be added as an authorized user. It's called "credit piggybacking." The user does not even have to let you use the card or even the account number. But you'll still benefit positively on your score because of their good credit history. A maneuver like this is a great boost to your credit. Especially if you're just starting your credit journey.

Pay your bills on time Late payments hurt and they hurt for 7 ½ years. That's how long it takes to come off your report. A payment missed by 30 days or more causes you to need to call the creditor immediately. Every month you miss after that hurts even more. Pay A.S.A.P if you want to start the process, lengthy process repair. You know the saying "An ounce of prevention Is worth a pound of cure." Yeah, that makes sense here. "On time pay prevention, prevents downward credit score destination." Remember that.

<u>Dispute credit report errors.</u> If you aren't going to do it, then don't make beef for it. Attempt to have bad marks on your credit removed immediately. It could cost you if a creditor believes you've missed a payment when you didn't.

<u>Deal with collections accounts.</u> Paying off two collections accounts removes the threat of being sued over the debt. You might get the collections agency to stop reporting the debt once you pay it. You can get others removed if they're too old or inaccurate to be listed.

<u>Use a secured credit card.</u> With this you can build or re-build your credit. This is a card backed by an upfront cash deposit. The amount you deposit is usually your credit limit. If you use it like a regular card and pay on time, then it will help to build your score.

<u>Get credit for rent and utility payments.</u> On time rent payments do two things. First, it keeps you off the streets. Lol. But also rent reporting services add them to your credit score. Although they are not considered by every scoring model, if a would-be creditor looks at your reports it can only help.

Add to your credit mix: An additional credit account that looks good may help your credit. Especially if it's the type you already have. A credit builder loan can be a low-cost option. Make sure the loan you're considering reports to all three credit bureaus. Or taking out a new credit card can also help. These things can help improve your credit mix as well as reduce your overall credit utilization by providing more available credit.

Now what I'm about to do for you is show you something that can help you go from "0 to 100 real quick," like Drake said but in this instance, we're referring to getting your "Business credit score" up there. Because that's the max. Come on and let me show you how to take it to the limit. I told you before, its levels to this, so let's get to the next one. Leveling up to Business credit. So, a business is an enterprising entity or organization that conducts professional activities. They can be commercial, industrial, or others. For profit businesses make money. Non-profit ones do it for the love of those they want to help, meaning for free. The ability to receive services or goods before payment is the definition of credit. Business credit allows you to borrow funds to buy products, goods, and services upfront and pay later. Sometimes, well often with interest.

Businesses come in 4 types. The most common are Sole Proprietorship, Partnership corporation, and S. Corporation. Later in the book I'll be discussing the difference and importance of using these or an LLC. For now, just focus briefly on

Business credit and the builders of your business's ability to use credit.

Business credit is your business's ability to navigate credit and use it to strengthen a business standing towards profitability. Your score influences your access to credit products. These include credit cards and loans. Your score gives indicators to vendors, suppliers, and all other creditors as to whether you pay your bills on time.

It takes 2 to 3 years to build satisfactory credit for a business. However, some lenders, or other financial institutions require only 1 year of a business operating venture to qualify for eligibility to receive funds. Business credit is important. It is part of your operating arsenal and part of your financial power and as with any power comes with a degree of responsibility. Places like Dun & Bradstreet, Experian, and Equifax allow you to check your business credit to make sure it's up to par.

Establish credit with companies that report trades. Not all companies do. But whichever creditors you use to pay them on time, every time.

Don't forget that the buy now-pay later is great for a short-term fix. But don't misuse that power because using it the right way as the tool it is, it will strengthen your position and ability to grow whatever business you decide to create. On the other hand, if you misuse it then it will turn from a power into a problem that will take you out of the game. Although something interest free does not mean that it is risk free. Be savvy enough to know the difference.

One major life changing stimulation is Artificial Intelligence (AI): refers to the simulation of human intelligence in machines that are programmed to think, learn, and problem-solve like humans. It encompasses various technologies and approaches, such as machine learning, natural language processing, and computer vision, to enable machines to perform tasks that typically require human intelligence. AI It's probably one of the biggest technological developments of our lifetime up there with computers but this is an AI assistant commonly used by people. It's the best one currently available without knowledge of coding and stuff. It's hundreds of times smarter than us as can search the entire web and world for info and seconds and compile it. You can have it sound like anything or anyone and summarize or do all your work. You can also use AI to help you word your disputes and help with the consumer laws. 'Dispute Panda' is an AI powered credit repaid website that help you with this process a lot faster than you doing it yourself. There is a small fee for this service.

Hey baby, put these business credit builders in your pocket and take them with you for later:

<u>Credit Strong</u>
- Offers credit builder accounts.
- Cash secured installment plan loan.
- You can cancel an account at any time, but you have to pay the loan off first. You will the money back.

## NAV

- Finds tools to build credit.

## Ecredable

- Reports to all 3 credit bureaus

## Uline – Business supplies

## Quill- Business supplies

## Grainger- Business supplies

Step off on the right foot.

- Establish your business.
- Register your business.
- Get your EIN.
- Open Business banking
- Buy business supplies/maintain positive relationship.
- Pay Early and on time.
- Focus on credit utilization.

CHAPTER 5

# A KEY TO WEALTH BUILDING. REAL ESTATE

INVESTING IN REAL ESTATE IS A WONDERFUL WAY TO invest in your future. Through Real Estate you can increase your ability to reach your financial goals. About $1.995 trillion is expected to be generated in revenue related to real estate in 2024 and that number will most likely increase every year.

No matter who you are, where you live or what you believe in you can use this avenue as a tool to create, build, and preserve your wealth. Demand for Real Estate is consistent one. Despite the economic factors that may influence the market and its demands. But even when the economy is in a slump and the number of buyers decreases, the opportunities for those that understand the pressure and market swings gain a very lucrative advantage.

To establish a solid understanding in the business of Real Estate you will need to stay focused and study before, during, and after every investment. My plan here is to introduce you to several ideas related to Real Estate investing. But before I do that, I want to drop a major jewel for you.

In the earlier chapters I gave you some game on how to clean up your credit history and build your FICO score. But maybe you've tried or will try, and things aren't moving like you need them to. Well, I have a solution to that. How about you just start all over? What I mean is that below you will be introduced to a remedy for your credit issues and that remedy is called an CPN/SCN.

To sum it up a CPN/SCN is a nine-digit number that can be used as your SSN. It will give you a clean credit history with the opportunity to build it the way you want.

1.  Go to http://www.stevenmorse.org/SSN/SSN.html this site will help you decide on the first set of numbers in your new social (for example: 123-???-????)

2.  http://www.ssa.gov/employer/sssnvhighgroup.htm this site will help you choose the second set of numbers (for example: (???-22????) After that you pick the last four numbers.

3.  http://www.verifico.com/app/strong-tower/cpn-ssn-validation/971?s=direct
    (This is the best site to check your # and make sure it's 100% clean and doesn't belong to anyone dead or alive) If it checks out you are good to go, if not, change the last four #'s and try again.

This CPN/SCN should not be used irresponsibly, nor should it be an excuse to not take care of your actual credit tied to your SSN, but it should be used as your stepping stone to financial freedom. You cannot pursue loans as well as lines of credit. Think of all the opportunities that come with that.

With little to no capital of your own, you can start your business in real estate investing. In the marketplace there are always private investors that have plenty of money to invest. Yet have little or no interest or ability to do the work or the deal themselves.

Profit from the "equity" build up can be built at the same time the property is naturally increasing in value. Market conditions and demand dictate this factor. This capital can be used to finance additional investments.

Multiple channels for profit exist that you can enjoy. Rather it's casual, first-time investor or even the experienced one, there is something for everyone to take advantage of. When you understand the variety of opportunities available, you can choose the deals that help you reach the goals you decide on at the fastest pace available.

Once you learn the basics, it is only a small jump to being able to understand the more complex ideas of the business. Which creates a process that can be repeated. This can be done on multiple types of properties. Profits increased considerably without you working harder to do so. There are "Tax Break" benefits to be had in Real Estate. You may need to consult with a tax professional for any details, but they are there. You can do things like write off certain business expenses for example, you can deduct the interest portion of mortgage payments.

Opportunities for Real Estate investing is all around you. With simple effort you can establish relationships with real estate professionals. You can also place your own ads to generate leads.

It's not complicated to market real estate. A for sale sign, direct mail campaign, or other simple techniques will do the trick. A flyer posted in the right place could potentially generate thousands of dollars in profit.

Wanna expedite an increase in your profits? Then build a power team. Establish solid relationships throughout your community and the business itself. These people can partner with you in investments or buy one of your properties. A solid team would include a good real estate agent, brokers, real estate lawyers, an accountant, tax expert, home inspector, a mentor, builders, and qualified contractors.

Owning and investing in real estate allows you to be in

a position to help others. You can alleviate the stress of an owner with a depressed property. Or you can assist a person struggling with debt. Like in a situation where the bank is threatening to take their home. You may be able to assist and help save their credit standing. The possibilities are endless.

You can use short- or long-term investment opportunities and strategies. These provide flexibility of choice. Then you can craft a schedule that matches your lifestyle and fits your needs. The entire world has gone virtual and so has real estate. Knowledge is key, you can use that from anywhere. Regardless of your current financial situation you can still get involved. There is many creative financing or buying approaches. Such as government programs, seller financing, lease options allow you to purchase properties with no money down.

Even when you have poor credit there are options available that will allow you to invest in Real Estate. Look into things like "wrap around mortgages," equity, financing, or partnering with other investors. Real Estate provides people with opportunities to profit and earn income. Creativity is key.

My suggestions to you are that you roll up your sleeves, strap on your boots, and get to work!

# CHAPTER 6

# THE SUCCESS OF GETTING FURTHER

NO ONE ON THE FACE OF THE PLANET HAS THE POWER TO control or decide the circumstances into which they were born. We do have the power of choice. Your future circumstances and life conditions will be determined using that power. What you will do with your own life is the question you must ask yourself daily. In this way you will become vigilant of and conscious of the choices you make. Choose a life of direction. Choose a life of prosperity. Choose a life of success. In all of it's forms.

Mastering a laser focus on your ability to keep things in perspective will allow you to make proper choices. The direction you are looking for dictates your focus, and life will consistently lead you along that chosen course.

If you are looking forward toward success and prosperity, then that's the direction you'll head. If you keep looking backward toward the past its likely, you'll just fall back on your old unproductive ways. Your focus and attention determine the direction you take. No one ever reached their destination while staring in the rear-view mirror. If you have ever driven a car, then you know that can be an accident waiting to happen. If you do not see what's coming right at you could be devastating or fatal to the whole trip.

In life there is always a silver lining to be found in any cloud of misfortune. Even the worst of circumstances have some aspects from which you can learn. Looking at the glass as "half-full" allows you to at least receive the gift of a lesson in these troubled times that will give you a possible new source of knowledge to draw from.

If you fell yesterday, have the strength to stand up today. Thomas Edison failed at making the light bulb over 100 different times. When asked about it he simply said:

"I did not fail over 100 times; I figured out over 100 different ways not to make a light bulb."

His comment illustrates a classic example of the "glass-half-full" perspective. You cannot fear or frown upon failure. Had he allowed himself to become self-defeated or overly discouraged by those initial failures, it's likely that all would still be in the dark. No one is perfect or wins all the time. There will be times when you just simply come up short. But it is in these times when the most successful people in the world find strength in their inner power within.

Persistence and resilience are key. Do not stop because of tiredness or failure. Stop when you are done. Do not give up before your breakthrough. Ever heard of "Chinese water torture?" It's the consistency of a simple drop of water against the forehead that has the power to drive you crazy. You can metaphorically allow life's challenges to do that to you. Or, with the power of your persistence, you can use it like that same drop of water that has the power to cut through stone and metaphorically you can cause the manifestation of your breakthrough.

Life without losses is life without learning. Losses only create regrets if you do not learn from them. So, always remember: "My losses are my lessons." A classic line used by those who have run into (usually), minor problems in their plans say, "One step forward, two steps back." This is a loser's way of thinking. A winner takes a step forward and may experience some hindrance, snag, or problem attempting to prevent their forward progress. In this situation the wise winner will "sidestep" and re-evaluate their plan of attack. Then after assessing the problem, they solve it, and keep moving forward. There is no back peddling, retreat, nor surrender. It's better to have tried and failed, than never to have tried at all.

'End Game Focus' allows nothing to distract or destroy you. Just remember to sidestep in those tense moments that may confront you, keep in mind that one failure doesn't cause the loss. It is the pattern of failures that does. So, in times of loss or failure, seek to find the flaw in the program that caused it. Then fix that.

A huge part of perspective is influenced by the way you speak. Phrases like: "I can't" "it's always something" "why me" never gets anybody anywhere or gets anything done. That type of speaking and thinking manifests failure into existence. The power of the subconscious mind exists and is strong enough to affect your reality. Have you seen the experiment in which a scientist spoke negative and positive messages to separate plants for 30 days? The plant subjected to negativity comments, turning deep brown and died, while the plant that was positively spoken to thrived. This experiment, replicated by various students across the world, underscores the impact of words on living organisms. Consider the profound effect negative self-talk can have on you, recognizing that as a human, your complexity far surpasses that of a plant.

Practice substituting all your "negative" speech, thoughts, and actions for the "positive" opposites. In this way you will create a pattern of positivity that will attract positive people, places, and opportunities into your life and immediate sphere. The pull of positivity is powerful. Think about that when you choose to surround yourself with other individuals.

Try to find people on the same page and positive story as you, people that have similar interests, goals, and direction in mind. Refer to this as being equally yoked dealing with like-minded people. Especially as you attempt to go, "All the way up."

Be careful then be discerning those you attempt to pull up with you. If you're a float on top and someone is beneath you are drowning. If you're not careful of that when you put your hand out to help, they can either grasp on to the positivity you offer and be pulled up out of a bad situation, or they can allow their overwhelming negativity to pull the both of you down to the bottom of Life's depths.

A negative person can be like a cancer. Their wicked thoughts, actions, attitudes, and outlooks can spread like Covid-19 just from them breathing that poison they spew in the mere presence of your otherwise health circle. The exchange of positive or negative energy is real. One way or another it will propagate out of control. To the point that it will affect anything and anyone around that energy. Even and especially you.

You can see the truth of this principle in the music industry. This is the reason that "opening acts" or "hyper-men" are used. They are used to build positive energy in the room. Creating that "In the zone" affect. Just look at the effect the crowd has on any sports team. Either positive or negative. You ever noticed how a "heckler" in the crowd can ruin any performance? It's the negative energy shift or exchange. Which can create an overload of fear, anxiety, or other unhealthy emotions to rub off. "One bad apple spoils the bunch." There's an actual science to that. So be careful to examine the ones you choose for your batch or team of individuals to associate yourself with.

Train, then dedicate yourself to a regimen of practice. Fine tune your technique. Practice certainly makes perfect because when you do something enough it becomes second nature. To the point where you don't even have to think about it. You just react according to what you have trained yourself to be or do. In the same way a body builder sculpts or molds his body to achieve the desired effect, you can do the same with yourself in terms of your mental outlook. You can also apply this to habits you wish to break by replacing them with new ones.

Understanding where to excel is just as important, if not more, as choosing what to excel in. For example, you're not going to perform country music at a rap concert. (Nelly might lol) or selling mixed drinks at church to function. "It's the best to go where you're celebrated and welcomed." Not just tolerated but really accepted and appreciated.

Seeking the proper venue for your talents, skills, abilities, or other infinities puts you in play in areas where similar individuals are attracted to and congregate. When destinies collide, moments of greatness are born. Being in the right place at the right time can fast track your success. Link up with or meet up with the movers and shakers in the fields or industry you choose to be connected to.

One moment, one blessing, one meeting, or connection is all you need for things to change. The power of one door opening can be the difference between the minor league to that of the majors. Knowing your place of position puts in direct line for you to be able to receive those associated benefits.

Want to try something impossible? I have a challenge for you. Try to please everybody. Forget about it. Never going to happen, because my attempt to please one person might be just the thing that makes someone else mad. Some people just will never be happy, unless it's only when someone else is miserable. The best thing you can do is get in the world where you fit in. Do the best you can by others with what you have to offer.

Not everyone will believe in you or be able to see your dream. That's alright. Although, they can't see the seed and know what it will become, they cannot deny the flower you will flourish into. You just must be sure to plant yourself in the most fertile soil possible. You cannot think that if you plant your seeds in the sand that it will grow. A little bit of common sense will tell you that if you plant your seed where similar plants grow well then chances are, you will thrive there as well. Find more qualified personnel if you desire better results.

One great advantage in these current times is the inter-connectedness of the world is through the internet and social media. Everything and everybody have gone virtual. I can be in the U.S of A and my presence can be felt anywhere in the world because of this valuable tool. With the right number of followers and friends you can make almost anything feel popular and seem valuable. You can find ways to make this translate into money as the bottom line. These days if you cannot concoct a creative way to generate some legal funding then you just don't want any.

Create a movement, a hashtag, or something else that has the potential to go viral. Just don't water down your possible influence. Be sure to portray the purity of your message or movement to the public. People love authenticity.

Who you are and what you represent or stand for matters. This speaks volumes about the person you are. Integrity means that even when no one is looking for your morals and values do not waiver. Having this trait and applying it will get you further than you can imagine. If people trust in your ability to further their own interest, then you have created immense value in yourself. One that others will pay to be associated with.

Many doors will open for you because of this. Options, tasks, outlets, and opportunities will be made more readily available. This is what happens once you've gained the confidence of the people.

Ever met someone who would lie, even if it were easier to tell the truth? This person is quickly defined as an untrustworthy scumbag. People respect and prefer the individual who is unafraid to convey a hard truth. Especially when a lie would be the easier option. You must find the courage to be that individual. There are no corners to be cut with that type of person. Despite whom might not like it.

When dealing with contracts, always dot your I's and be sure to cross all your T's. Be certain to incorporate the language of any contracts presented for your signature. As well as be sure that you include all the language of eventualities needed to cover your own interest in any contract. Time is money. Be on time. Keep your mind. And stand on principles. Be realistic. Use what you have to get where you are trying to go. Cherish your relationships, all of them. Use every opportunity you must network. Be gracious, never greedy. Gratefulness goes a long way. Also, always give back. Remember, life is a journey of peaks and valleys. So, the ones you see on the way up are the same ones you'll pass again on the way back down. And above all don't practice ego defensive projection. This is when you see your own undesirable traits in others, while denying them in yourself. This is the character of a selfish person whose only concern is the defense of their own ego. Having integrity and being honest are two great components utilized in building good character. Character is how the world views you and what is used to measure you by just like a person with integrity maintains that even when no one is looking, character is the building blocks of who you are when everyone else is who they are. No matter the reason, rationale, or circumstance. Although others may behave in a certain way or dishonesty, you remain the same. There are no grey areas involved.

Maintaining a regimen of learning and strengthening your mind is important. The act of learning never stops. No one knows everything. Every day is another opportunity to gain experience or discover something new. Make sure you develop your critical thinking and keep your critical thinking skills sharp. Even In your down time, pray and stay connected spiritually. You are even able to play games such as Sudoku, chess, crosswords, brain games, and puzzles. These sorts of activities activate and stimulate that region of your brain in a fun and entertaining way.

The goal is to become the smartest person in the room. Yet you must maintain enough finesse. Humility, and tact not to let everyone know it. This idea serves to provide you with just a bit of an advantage. Keep an ace in the hole and hold your cards close to the chest.

Never limit your information input. You never know what might spark a profitable idea or when this current information may turn out to be otherwise useful. Learn a little bit about everything. This way you'll have a reference point to be able to participate in nearly any topic of conversation. Then people can't talk over your head and learn how to learn.

Read books regularly. This helps to increase your vocabulary. A broad vocabulary assists in understanding. The definition of a single word can color or change the complexion or meaning of an entire sentence.

And when I say read, I refer to the types of material that millionaires and billionaires read. Information of importance. Like the world news, reports on finance, the stock market, economics, coding or real estate. Even speeches or interviews with world leaders or the moguls of business. Reality TV and celebrity gossip magazines can only keep you updated on the reality of the fantasy being created by characters in order to sell the product of an entertaining personality to the world. Keep it real and pay attention to real life. Don't be surprised if you find out that sometimes the truth is strange, and more entertaining than fiction. Especially since more often than not there exists a book on any field or endeavor that you wish to excel in. Reading them can only help you get to the bag faster. Now what could be more entertaining than that?

Finally let me leave with a quote by "A Fallen Son Rises" that may help you contemplate and keep your position and situation in perspective.

"Because you are there, the world changes. So, in some regard, you must be where you are, for the world to be where it is. meaning, the combination of factors that align by, and because of your presence, creates an equational reality expressed by situation 1 outcomes. Translation, nothing is by accident, all things are connected."

# V.I.P TAKEAWAYS

_____

_____

_____

_____

_____

_____

_____

_____

_____

_____

# CHAPTER 7

# BUSINESS 101

---

*"The enterprise of the supply chain of Life"*

---

AN ENTERPRISE IS DEFINED AS "A PROJECT THAT REQUIRES boldness and energy" The business term "supply chain" has a term within it called the "fulfilment" process. These are the stages a product channels through from conception to the customer or consumer.

In life at its core business is a service, it's the "giving of oneself in a manner that brings fulfillment to another by supplying something produced out of your mind as a product into a service.

Business in its imagery gives us a picture of giving, serving, sharing, making oneself useful for humanity. It never can co-exist with selfishness. Quite simple, one can never truly succeed in full potential in business being a selfish person because the very principle favors a giver rather than a taker.

Therefore, now let's discuss the process of the supply chain in a business, which takes the form of several shades in. These stages aim to provide comfort, upliftment, and bring joy, happiness, and fulfillment to humanity.

The principles are spiritual in nature, that which a man sows he will also reap. A product is first concerned in the mind in seed form. Seed represents the inception of an idea, vision, or purpose. This is the highest stage of the supply chain, in that it is connected to the creator or master of the product, one who is the owner of the seed, or idea, vision or purpose.

The prefix "pro" comes with the meaning "beforehand" "primitive, "embryonic" in nature. Primitive meaning "belonging" to the earliest stages of development. In our context It conveys at the "mental level," in the mind.

Embryo carries the meaning of seed, which is a product in the mind of its master or creator before it is produced. Expert or creator of a product is the highest beneficiary of the fruits its produced. This is where we get the term "intellectual property" from or copywrite and trademark which is legal patents that signify ownership, creator, or expert.

In the music business they say "own your masters" … Truly because you are the creator or master of the lyric and should be the highest beneficiary. Creator or master is the first fruits of business and service toward humanity.

Creator (thought) of car, truck, book, internet, app, beverage, shoe, skincare, house, corp. etc.

Now we move into our next stage of the "supply chain fulfillment process," we come into manufacturing of the product, which should seem to be that the product is the same persons. Could be but not always.

The product can proceed from the mind of a creator when conceptualized yet be manufactured or produced by another.

The lyrics come by way of the creator or master of the one who delivered the expression from his mind, but the song is usually composed by the producer.

The house is built by the construction contractors, but the vision of the home comes from the developer. Tesla came from the visionary mind of Elon Musk, but he did not manufacture the first car himself.

However, the manufacturer is the second stage in the supply chain, fulfillment process, therefore let's investigate the word manufacturer and obtain a better thought on this stage in the process.

Note, the manufacturer receives hefty compensation as well in that they are the ones who bring the product into fruition for the people to receive the benefit. They sit near to creator or master of thought. God was man's creator as well as manufacturer wherefore God has blessed man with "mind," and the intellectual ability to take on the form of creator and master himself in things pertaining to the life cycle for the benefit of humanity.

This is why creator, master, and manufacturer receive the highest level of the blessing in the supply chain fulfillment process, because man acts as God intended him to do so create for the well-being of others.

Looking into the word manufacturer in its imagery we see the importance it holds in the "supply chain fulfillment process" of production, as the product makes its way to and for a service among people.

The website defines manufacturer as "to work up into form." In its imagery the word man-u-facture is defined on the website as a "a male servant or attendant." The word fact in man-u-fact-urer is defined on the website as "To reproduce or manifest something that actually exist." That exist where? In the mind of creator or master of thought, idea, vision, or purpose.

Therefore, we can say the manufacturing, process indicates, the second stage of servanthood, the first being a servant by way of his mind, the second his hand, in bringing a service to humanity by bringing into manifestation the actual physical creation from conception creation into a product useful in an area that brings fulfillment.

At the business level this stage is just as important as creator or master of the seed of thought concerning the product produced. Without a servant there will no service and without service the product lays dormant in its primitive stage.

Manufacturing is also the stage where the product is produced on a mass scale to react the need or want of the people.

This is the fruitful stage as the servant prepares the service for the marketplace.

The website defines "market" as "people assembled," A body of existing buyers for specific goods or services. The word "mark" in market brings us closer to the imagery of our business 101 context as the website defines "mark" as "a visible expression," "A token or indication, a device or symbol serving to identify ownership."

Therefore, manufacturing is the stage set for preparing the goods or service for the people as the manufacture produces the physical manifestation of the product itself as a token of ownership by the creator or master of thought. The manufacturer receives a wholesome benefit for giving themselves to such a service or labor as a servant for the people.

Token is defined as "something serving to represent a feeling." Wherefore in the business 101 process the conception of Idea or vision is a token of his respect, honor, and love for humanity to render his mind of service to think of such.

It then the process of manufacturing becomes a further stage of honor, respect, and love as the people render themselves of service to bring the product to use.

It's not a wonder one is greatly compensated in the area of business, not just from the physical product but the product or service being tied to one's intentions, to "busy" himself in an endeavor for the sake of someone else, which is a selfless act.

Not all people approach business at this level and may still be compensated for a product, but nowhere near as when someone approaches business with the right heart and attitude of mind beyond making money.

Spiritual law, universal law, rewards intentions. Good or bad, therefore, one can hinder their progress with the wrong intentions. With the right intentions you will "super-charge" your progress.

There is a level of love that comes from a heart that speaks to serve others. Love is always compensated. It's a universal language. It attracts value, whether it's money, relationships, or good health often, all three. Therefore, life is a business, you are a business. Love is synonymous with giving, love produces, selfishness destroys.

Now we come into the next process of the "fulfillment process" which is sales, retail, the time the product becomes useful when the consumer or customer is fulfilled.

The imagery in these words conveys to us the meaning of this stage in the supply chain. The word "tail" in re-tail is defined as "a final concluding part" or "the lower position" sale is defined as "an offering" "an opportunity." Opportunity is defined as a "favorable occasion."

It's at this point that the sale represents a favorable occasion whereby a product has been produced for the benefit of another person and has been offered in visible expression for use as the consumer or customer is fulfilled.

Fulfilled is defined as "to satisfy." A customer is synonymous with a consumer. Customer is defined as "a person who receives service from another, while consumer is defined as "to use" expend or absorb. It connotes in actions that correspond to the desires, wants, and needs.

This stage is the lowest point of the supply chain, in that the fulfillment process is complete, the person is satisfied and has benefited from the service of another.

However, it's also the lowest point in the process because the benefit of the consumer is nowhere near the benefit of the person who comes up with the idea, master, manufacturer, or engage in the business of sales to the one who forwards the goods or services to the consumer or customer. Each stage has its own level of compensation and reward. Unfortunately, consumers get the short end of the stick because consumers don't really provide a service or work like others in the process. Jesus said, "It is more blessed to give than to receive."

Truly because it's the compensation element of the heart of a servant that the universe rewards. Furthermore, everyone will play consumer at many points in life, and should joyfully do so knowing they are taking part in compensating a servant. But the question is "Will one play servant?"

A businessperson is a servant, his creation or his service is for people and he reaps the fruits of his nature. However, one must decide what field he will play in most regarding his life.

Will he manifest seeds as creator/master of thought and vision? Will he plant and prepare the soil for production as manufacturer? Will he gather crops to bring to the people as sale representative or will he be content eating from the hand of other men? Will he get served only, or will he serve becoming a servant also? Man was made to serve. A child gets served up until the point of adulthood then he himself is expected to become a servant.

Will he make the truck, or will he buy the truck and render it a useful service for people, or will he just drive the truck?

Will he develop a plan for a house, or will he build the house, or will he buy the house and render if a service for another, or will he just live in it?

Will he make clothes, or will he buy the clothes and resell the clothes rendering a service for people, or will he just wear the clothes?

Each has its own reward system, choose your reward. Nothing is better than the offer if you have peace, happiness, good health and wholesome relationships. Nevertheless, a servant is "enterprising"/rendering a service makes people useful for and to each other, It employs people and take part in God's idea of family and community.

# CHAPTER 8

# BECOMING A GENERATIONAL THINKER

OF YOUR HARD WORK, DEDICATION, AND DEVOTION TO the goal of accomplishment the question now becomes, "What will you be remembered for?" The answer to this may require some serious thought. But it Is important that we as individual humans thinks about these sorts of things. Because at some point, a person must make the decision, then the conscious effort to make their life a vital and important contribution to all of humanity. So, what legacy shall you leave?

At the very least you should want to leave behind the blueprint and foundation for what may be used by those that you love, and are a part of your lineage, the tools to build a fountain of "Generational Wealth". Every day the chasm separating the "Haves" and the "Have Nots" steadily grows as the wealth gap increasingly widens between the two. One of your life goals should include some sort of financial connection or bridge to the other side that your family may utilize.

One thing is for certain and that is the fact that the one promise to human beings is that this life will not last forever. Yet although your allotted measure of time is indeed limited, there is no telling how your bloodline may go. Your efforts today may very likely make a difference in how their lives progress and develop in the future. Access to "Generational Wealth" is an advantage or head-start that many not able families have benefited from in our society in the past. And will continue to benefit from it in the future.

To begin the process of becoming a generational thinker you need to make decisions about the direction and purpose of your life with this thought factored into the equation. Do not allow yourself to get into a comfort zone and simply stay stuck there. You do not want to go through life before you find out or realize why. Use the challenges in life that you will confront and overcome to reveal to you the power of abilities you've had deep inside of you all along.

One thing for sure is the fact that there is not any more land being created. That is why I personally try to acquire as much as I am able. Real estate is a big part of generational wealth that can be passed down in the family for potentially centuries to come.

Also get in the practice of buying items of value that have the potential to only increase in value over time. Most of us have the tendency to waste wealth by purchasing things that isn't worth the paper it's printed on or will otherwise not even be worth the price you paid to own it three years down the line. There is a definite difference between an asset and a liability. Know the true value of the things that you seek to purchase and whether it will either increase or depreciate with the passage of time.

Master the language of money, and then excel in articulating it. This involves educating your children and loved ones on becoming adept at the skills of creating, building, and managing credit. Credit is King. Do invest in it early and often. Do this by teaching your children the importance of managing money. As well as to give the principals involved with protecting their credit. Use their technique of making them an authorized used on your account to provide them with a head-start with credit-building.

Budgeting is necessary. Never use the excuse for spending money on frivolous purchases simply because you have the money to do it. Most of us get in the bad habit of buying more just because we perceive we have more to spend. There Is no shame in living within your means. Too many of us buy more than we can afford simply to give the appearance to others that we are of a status higher than we truly are or that we live this ultra luxurious lifestyle. But I have an idea that may help you out a little bit. The next time that you believe that you have a few thousand dollars or even a couple hundred dollars to spend, do the opposite. Save it. Find yourself an interest-bearing account and stuff the money in there. If you just must spend the money then fine, find a true asset to buy instead. Try that for 2 years and see how much money on some designer clothes and red bottom shoes are nice to have if you can honestly afford them. Otherwise, you are taking away some of your own power and potential to develop "Generational Wealth" and are donating it to the pool of wealth that will sustain the designer of those same clothes and his lineage not your own.

Education helps to provide a boost in economic status and upward mobility. Even if you haven't been to college, encourage your children to go. Consider the money you spend on their tuition as an investment in the future of not only your kids but also those of the generations that follow. It is a studied fact that children with parents who are college graduates are more likely to become college graduates themselves. This is where dividends of your initial investment in school fees will be paid. Generationally. You must realize, that like it or not, there are certain classes of individuals in this country, for historical reasons, which have become part of, and trapped within the merciless cogs of machine that has created unseen pitfalls and systematic cycles that maintain their repressed position by design. At present, the only perceivable tool available for those individuals to change their status or mitigate these factors, is economic advancement toward establishing Generational Wealth. Point Blank Period.

Until you learn to become a generational thinker, you will always make foolish choices. Those ignorant choices serve to only have the affect or perpetuating this current system of proportionality and by proxy helps to maintain the inequitable status that some individuals find themselves in and labeled as secondary.

Casting pearls to swine or living just to have bread for today are the actions of the individual who forgets the consequences of their actions and poor decisions most certainly will affect the next generation. We must think wisely people. Make sound choices so that it will be celebrated in those generations to come that freedom and forward development came because of you.

# V.I.P TAKEAWAYS

---

---

---

---

---

---

---

---

---

---

# CHAPTER 9

# MENTAL BREAK DOWN

HOT AS FISH GREASE. THAT'S THE ONLY WAY THAT I CAN describe the heat of the summer sun as it beats down mercilessly on my scalp. The buckets of sweat that rolled down my back in a torrent like a rainstorm didn't do anything to cool me off like it should have either. For real it was so hot outside that it almost felt like it was real fish-grease sliding down my back and sticking to every inch of my exhausted body. Plus, every single muscle I knew I had and even the ones that I didn't even know existed hurt beyond description.

"Let's Go Ladies! Move it! Wait, as a matter of fact I can't even call y'all ladies. That would be giving y'all too much credit. My ninety-year-old grandmother can move faster than this! I'll tell you what! Either you can pick up the pace, or you know what? Well, start all over again. Then we'll see how you little knuckle heads like that!"

That was the coach. As usual he was screaming at us like the mad man me and the other players on my high school football team thought he was. Every time he opened his mouth aint nothing come out of It but form harsh words, insults and bad breath.

"Oh! I get it. You lil jokers must think I'm playing huh? Okay. Last chance. I better see some speed, otherwise ill run you little punks until your feet bleed" Coach said then pulled the stopwatch out of his pocket then picked up the spit drenched whistle from around his neck and began to blow it the way he loved to do so much. It probably smelled like wet butt. The same way his breath usually did.

"Man, I'm sick of this fool." I mumbled just loud enough to myself and enough to be heard by my teammate beside me.

"You too? Man, this idiot is about to make me quit. Playing for this team is starting not to be worth the headache." My teammate said in a mumble as he kept striding with me. The two of us mumbled because the last thing we wanted to do was to let the coach hear us complaining.

"Facts Bro!" I said with more emphasis than sound.

The two of us, along with the entire team, were running side by side, in full equipment, in the hot summer sun already 6 miles, he told us to run. All because somebody didn't run a play the way he said that they should. Coach had a philosophy:

If one of us messed up then we all paid the price. And this was only part of it.

"Left-Right! Left-Right! Good God! How hard can it be!? You little idiots think you're so smart do you!? Well, try and figure out how to do this right at least! I bet you fools can't think your way out of a wet paper bag! Now let's go! Otherwise, we will start all over again from the top!" Coach screamed until his little bubble-eyes nearly popped out of his head and every vein of his face bulged. He looked like he was about to have a stroke. Spit foamed at the side of his mouth like a rabbit dog.

"Bro 2" My teammate whispered.

"What's up?" I said from the corner of my mouth while breathing heavily from the exertion of the run.

"Man ... I feel sorry for that fool's wife." My teammate said between strides.

"Why you say that?" I asked then looked over at him.

"Well, first of all, I've seen his wife, she's fine. As bad as she is I don't know how in the world his troll looking self-ended up with her." He said with a smile then wiped the seat off his brow.

"You right about that. At least if he had a little bit of paper, I might could understand it. But other than that, I don't get it. He's definitely as broke as a bag of glass." I said then shook my head at the thought."

"Yeah. That might make sense. But, then again, I don't think that all the money in the world would be enough to compensate or help that poor women deal with her real problem." He said as a slight smile creased his face.

"Her real problem?" I said then looked at him dead on as we ran.

"Yea Bro. Come on man. Don't sit there and act like you ain't never smelled that man's breath. You and I both know that his tongue probably smells like a baby diaper. That fool mouth smells like a full Coachella port-a-potty. How is that poor woman is supposed to kiss that S-H? EWW!" He said, then started one of those contagious type of giggles.

When it hit me, I couldn't take it. And neither could a couple of other players near us that had heard us talking even though we thought that we were being quiet. I almost stumbled as the laughter slowly began to spread through us all. The moment that coach started to blow on that stupid whistle of his like a train is approaching a railroad crossing I knew right then we messed up.

"Everybody stop! Right now! Do not move another inch!" Coach screamed at the top of his lungs.

"Aw … man … here we go." I mumbled to myself then sucked my teeth.

When I stood still where I was, I could only fight hard to suppress my laughter. Watching coach run toward the section of the field where I was made my attempt to stop laughing twice was as difficult. For real, that man looked like a little, mad, pot-bellied piglet. His stomach jiggled like a bag full of Jello. And his shirt rolled up from that movement far enough that you could see every nasty roll and stretch mark.

"You simple minded Moot a scooter. Do your little tight

pants wearing, no money having, no "cookie" getting idiots find something funny about this!" Coach screamed as he ran up to us with what looked like murder in his eyes.

"Sir! No Sir!!" My team spoke in unison military style, just the way that he expected us to. The problem was that there were till snickers and giggles amongst the ranks.

"Got Daggit!" Jesus freaking Christ! You little mentally challenged knuckle heads must think that I'm as stupid as you are or you must think that I'm deaf. That's it! You know what would really be funny? Drop down! Get me some!!!" coach said with the tone, demeanor, and the rumble of voice like a real live drill sergeant.

That was the coach's way of instructing us to drop down into position on the ground so that we could experience one of his most favorite punishments. An exercise called "Six inches." That's when we'd lay on our backs with our feet extended out in front of us exactly "six inches" off the ground. Then, he'd make us hold that position for what seemed like an eternity. Man, I can remember the last time that he'd made us do that my stomach felt like I'd ripped something inside. It almost gave me a Hernia.

"Man I'm sick of this fool for real Joe." One of the players near me said as he laid a few feet down from me in obvious pain. Unfortunately for him though, coach must've heard him too.

"Ooooh Yeah!!!!" Coach said while sounding like the machoman randy savage. "Yes Lord I got me one!"

Coach ran right over to the dude near us who had made the mistake of opening his mouth just a bit too loud. When coach got up to him, he kneeled down right in front of the poor guy. Then he got close enough to his face that their lips almost touched. Ewwww ... (emoji-nasty face.)

"Boy, do you think something is funny? Or do you got something you wanna tell me?" Coach screamed right in his face as drool dripped out of his mouth on to the poor boy's face that probably smelled like toilet water fresh after a session of diarrhea caused by some bad Mexican food.

"Sir! No sir!" The boy screamed while obviously holding his breath with a look on his face that looked like he was ready to throw up.

"Yes you do. Go ahead. Be a man and say it to my face. That's alright. I know what it is. You don't like me do you? And you don't like how I handle you little slow head jokers. Good ... But you know? If you don't like it then ... Get off my team!!!!"

That was it coach screamed so loud and so much foam bubbled out of his mouth that the poor dude couldn't take no more. All he could do was to roll over onto his side to save himself the tart-tongue-tornado that coach had whipped up out of his mouth. Next, coach smiled, stood up, then prepared to make an announcement.

"Let me tell of you little half-wit punks something. I see you lil dudes come out here every week with your faces all bent up like you got toothache. Looking at me like you might want to try your hand with the old man.

I got a little grey in my beard. So I know how you little jokers are. You may think you got the UPS and can beat my old tail. And you know what? You might can. I see you dudes and get up under that bench and the gym and can lift more pounds off that bench-press rack then, I weigh. And that's cool. But, mentally, I'm the Olympic weightlifter. And I'd go mike Tyson Punch-out style on your little dim-witted brains. I'd beat all your brains into a mental pulp!!!"

When I heard the coach say those words, they were probably the best things that ever came out of that nasty filthy smelling mouth of his. I believe that was the point when I realized the importance of being the smartest person in the room. Except I wasn't gonna do like he did and tell everybody. I'd have a little bit more class than that. I planned to keep that as my little secret and keep the advantage intelligence would give me over other people to myself. But just this one time I'll let you in on a couple of little secrets that just might help give you a slight advantage over the competition. But before I tell you, first you need to understand that you can have all the knowledge in the world, but if you don't apply it then it means nothing. You might as well be as sense-less as coach thought we were.

As we have heard so many times. It's about not just strengthening but keeping all 3 elements; a strong mind, body, and spirit. The mental (brain) staying sharp (thinking) the physical keeping body in shape, workout, and the spiritual staying connected to the source.

# V.I.P TAKEAWAYS

_____

_____

_____

_____

_____

_____

_____

_____

_____

_____

# CHAPTER 10

# WHAT'S NEXT? WHERE TO START? TAKE A T-CAB UPTOWN

THE NEXT THING FOR YOU TO DO IS TO GET IN THE HABIT of making decisions that benefit you now and in the long term. Be certain that those decisions aren't based on your feelings for the moment. Never make permanent decisions based on temporary feelings. Because either you produce results that translate into profits and success, or you produce excuses that only justify and attempt to explain away failures. So, to stay away from failure pull away from it by taking a t-cab uptown, met a physically speaking.

Alight. Let's cut to the chase and get to the meat of the

dish first. T-cab is a simple acronym that stacks thought s-consequences-actions-belief. This is a good place to start if you're wondering where to begin because this acronym as a reminder helps to train your brain to be conscious of certain important principles.

Simply put, your thoughts can have consequences (either positive or negative), that are based off your actions. All of which are influenced by your own personal belief systems. So, when your T-cab is focused on proper direction then you are pointed toward achieving, or yielding positive results and consequences in your life. It's that simple.

Would you like to direct your T-cab towards the path to which you can use to up your personal and/or business credit dramatically? Well, start your engines. Don't tell nobody but, Shhhh …, I got a little secret that can help to cause a positive point swing on your credit report to something like 200 points in your favor.

Look into the exact same method that the banks, auto dealers, and property managers use as a technique to add personal loans and leases to your personal credit report. Research the use the U.C.C (uniformed commercial code) on how to place trade references on your report. Article 9 of the commercial code deals with secured transactions, any loan, lease, rental, or purchase where collateral is used to secure terms. Credit bureaus are connected to a public filings database that updates every 24-72 hours. Be diligent and find out one of the big secrets that some well-known credit gurus use to build their customer's credit.

"Are we there yet?" I don't know but let's take our T-cab and bend this corner. Maybe we can look at how stocks and trading can be used to play with some numbers. You remember what Jay-z said about those don't you? "Men lie, women lie, but numbers don't," so let's count and see. Because one plus one aint never gonna add up to three.

If you don't know nothing about trading like I didn't, then take the same "son course" that put me up on game. It dumbs it down so perfectly that anybody can get it. It's a total of 2 hours that are straight to the point. The app called "Gum Road" is for the course. This other app called "robin hood" is for trading. When you get some down time, simply set up an account. Try to do it during the trading hours between 9:30 am to 4:00 pm.

The app is user friendly and fun to use. In no time you'll get the "bag" up to a nice amount. After taking this course called "trade with loon" that has 4 parts, I took 7 thousand dollars and ran it up to 80 grand in one month. FACTS. That just lets you know that this is a sure thing with guaranteed potential. All it takes is for you to make maybe 3 to 4 trades before you catch on like crazy.

Now, we got one last stop on our ride uptown. And that's pulling our T-cab in front of a nice piece of real estate. Come on, let's pull over and have us a look.

Over the years I've been hit with a lot of questions about where to start the journey toward real estate ownership and property development. So let me give you a couple of good options and easy points to start with. These are the types of little nudges in the right direction that I like to offer people.

If you don't have a lot of money, or even bad or no credit you can still get in the game. First, go to a lawyer and start an L.L.C (Limited liability cooperation). It's inexpensive. Don't panic. Next, seek out lenders that provide what they call a "No Doc." Loan. With a no doc loan this means documentation-no credit. You can use one of these to fund a construction or property. But they require 20% up front for the loan amount you wish to borrow 100 grand to fund your project, then you are responsible for coming up with 40 grand to receive the loan.

Another avenue you could write your T-cab down is toward what they call a "Hard money" lender these private institutions are labeled as "Hard Money" Lenders because the interest rates are substantially larger. We're talking anywhere between 12 to 20% of the total loan amount. Plus, you must provide 3 to 5 percent of the loan amount up front. But if your credit score rates at a 620 or better than that its likely that you can secure this deal. The closing costs of any property sold will have to be covered by you as well. This can mean an additional 5 to 10 thousand range to start.

The advantage of using a hard money lender is that securing funding is easier and faster because the larger interest rates are a motivating incentive for the lenders profit margin. The disadvantage is that you're on the clock to pay back the money at a higher rate than usual. But in most cases, you can still make money within the allotted period they give you. It could be done properly in even something like 2 months on average. Because once you two Qualified Real Estate Agent to list the property on the M.L.S (Marketing Listing Scroll), it will usually get sold within a week or so. After which the closing people will calculate the amount, the lender should receive. You'll get the rest.

Are you looking for less hassle? Great, then let's cruise the T-cab down to less a busier street. One called, wholesaling "Distressed homes" at the corner of "cheap price lane."

A home in distress is one that is facing foreclosure, tax liens, or set up for auction for a variety of other reasons. You can acquire these properties for little to no out of pocket costs. This will enable you to provide these properties at wholesale prices to known investors at a percentage of actual value to make a quick flip. You basically make money by simply assuming then re-assigning a contract. This requires no money. Only time, attention, and foot work.

Want to keep a property, or two. Many teach fix and flip; I teach fix and keep. Rehab and build are the way. You can take one of the distressed properties you acquire, fix it, refinance it with a bank at a lower mortgage rate, move up, rent it out for a stream of monthly positive cash flow.

Now do me a favor. Take these jewels, stuff them in your back pocket, and be really, really, quiet about it. Shhhhh ... :-P and ;-) :-D

# V.I.P TAKEAWAYS

_____

_____

_____

_____

_____

_____

_____

_____

_____

_____

# IN THE END...
# REMEMBER TO WIN!

THE FORMULA FOR SUCCESS, BY ANY DEFINITION, IS A simple equation: Input + Output = outcome. So, with that being said, your net worth and status in life is based solely on your energy. Always be conscious of the fact that your energy. Always be conscious of the fact that your energy your initial investment. The energy that you focus on any endeavor is pledged as collateral for every exchange and cash outs to produce whatever is needed to produce the results that you seek.

With the power of focus you can live a life of power. Being focused means concentrating on your purpose. The actual and underlying reason why you do whatever it is that you choose to utilize to achieve your ultimate goals. To do this, you must at all costs avoid dilution. By this I mean beware of distraction because this can cause you to lose sight of your target.

A good example of something that may become a distraction is chasing the distraction is chasing the desires of the heart. Everyone has a "hearts desire." Most often it is tied to and intertwined with a romanticized version or image of the way they wish, dream, want or "desire" their life to be. Which isn't necessarily a bad thing, you just have to be aware of the fact that anything tied to or compelled by your deepest desires are attached to emotions. We all know how emotions can cloud your vision and affect the way you see any situation. But, walking in your calculated and concentrated purpose is patent, strong, richly favored, and brings deep satisfaction to your soul. The purpose inspired "Hearts Desires" does this.

Sometimes we may desire more, or to do more than we are capable of having or doing. Ever heard the expression: "Your eyes are bigger than your stomach?" This means that just because we want something because we see that it looks good to have doesn't mean that it will fit exactly where we try to put it and if we force it to fit our place or our lives, it could cause more pain than pleasure in the long run. Everything that looks "good" isn't necessarily "good for you."

You'll find that often people do this when they try to "wear too many hats," or otherwise assume too many responsibilities at once. The danger in "trying to do everything" will result in you actually "doing nothing at all." This why the richest and most successful people in the world understand the need for and the power of "Delegation." Let me give you an example of what I mean.

Okay I'm about to build a house. This is what I want. And I know exactly how I want it to look inside and out. So, since I have the "desire" to make it happen, and now the responsibility for it that I've given myself, then now I'm the one that's charged with getting it done. Perfect. But the problem is, I don't have a clue about doing any of the work on the house that needs to be done. I mean that I haven't hammered a nail in my life or lifted a screwdriver, and the only "pipe" I know how to lay is in the bedroom (emoji-tongue out), If you know what I mean, so, we got a situation.

Fortunately for me though, I understand the power of "Delegation" and how to use that skill to actualize the dream that I "desire" to see. This is because, as the "leader" of the situation I know that since no one person is good at everything, then I must be smart enough to know what it is that I can do, and that which I can't. So, after I've done all that I can, the next thing I must do is find these people who can do the parts of the job that I can't so that in the end the vision will be realized and complete.

So, in this case, the vision is this house that I'm responsible for building and thus "desire" to see. In order to get this picture out of my mind and onto the landscape in the world I've chosen I need plans to follow. I don't have a clue how to write them so of course I hire the architect that does a house needs a foundation to stand on, and sew age lines placed even before that, so I delegate these jobs to the professionals who are good at what they're good at. I follow this same "Delegation" skill to have the frame built, the electrical wired, the Insolation done, the "out of the bedroom" pipes laid :'-) :-D, the HVAC installed, the dry wall hung, roof done, windows placed, tiles placed, and then get the carpet placed and painted. And Viola! I've built the house.

A good leader recognizes the potential of all the players on his team. They understand how and where to utilize the skills that these individuals are the masters of. This, if done correctly, can be likened to the conductor at the symphony directly each instrument section into the perfect harmony that causes the goal at the end. A standing ovation.

Now, right off the bat, let's get something understood about being "Leader." Or better yet, a good leader. And to be a great leader, this requires a certain understanding. Along with particular skill set that will be required to get the job accomplished. A good leader is like the king on the chess board. Well, not even. It's like being the player over the chess board. The true leader is the one that sees the larger vision, the whole picture. In this sense they control even the king. The great leader knows the exact abilities of every piece on the board. As well as knowing where, when, and precisely how to utilize those abilities in order to achieve the end result. And that is to win. Point. Blank. Period.

Everyone "wants" to be the boss. But everyone can't or shouldn't be. Maybe you lack those particular qualities needed in order to properly or effectively be the boss of other people. Leadership is still a form of servitude. A good leader is also a good servant and there is something that you get out of serving that you can't receive from watching. But even if you aren't qualified to be the "Boss" of others you still have other great and important qualities to offer the world. So, the least you can do is be the "Boss" of yourself.

Discipline and self-control are skills necessary to develop in order to be the "Best Boss" of yourself. These attributes are not enemies to you, but rather they are trusted friends and the companions that are here to assist and guide you up the road toward forward progression in every area of your life. Hebrews 12:11 says: No Discipline seems pleasant ... but it produces a great harvest of righteous trains you ... "

Hardships and trials teach and train. Perhaps a particular loss you've experienced or may in the future may be the lesson of life you could need to progress forward. A life without loss is a life without learning. The only regret that comes from a loss is when the experience isn't learned from. One mantra you must always recite to yourself is that: "My losses are my lessons." In this way you will always be reminded these learned lessons are developing you into the masterpiece that you were destined to become.

Don't be "one in a million," be "one of a kind," and know that you already are. There is no competition at being you. "Do you," Like they say because there is no one on the face of the planet that can do you better than you. Aint no sense in trying to be like anybody else, because in reality, you simply can't. The information coded into the very strands of your D.N.A has made you unique and one of a kind. Face it and embrace it.

Always remember that the power of the promise is in the plan. Don't just run off with the promise without sticking around for the plan. Having a vision is the very first step to forming any plan. Where do you want to be at the end of the day; the week; the year; 5 years; 10 years; etc.? Of course, I encourage every one of us to start off small. But keep in mind that the one who sees the furthest and plans toward the bigger accomplishments is the one who plans toward bigger success. It's like chess.

You've got to walk before you can run. Actually, crawling comes first. So, make a list of short term and long-term goals you wish to accomplish. Start with day to day or week to week goals to begin with. Before long you'll begin to realize that your daily accomplishments, when structured right, will put you in a direct line to accomplish the weekly ones. There is when you take the time to reflect on what and how you've accomplished these goals, and also recognize and highlight positive patterns you notice emerge.

The roots determine the fruits. Your focus and determination define the source of your life. Stick religiously to your plans and keep your thoughts forever focused on that. Your life will go in the direction of your most dominant thoughts. Be wise enough to be careful with what you do in your private time because you will see the fruits of these thoughts in your public life. The un-seen will be seen and our faith can manifest it in our lives. Faith the currency of heaven. With this is how we can pay for the things that the natural eye cannot see. Take the risk and speak good things into existence in your life. Then have faith in the future and allow that to produce obedience in the present.

Yesterday is history, tomorrow is a mystery, and today is a gift. Which is why it's called the "present." Don't waste or squander a minute of it. Not even a single one of the 86,400 seconds that were given each day. Sow the right seeds in the right areas of your life today so that you can reap the rewards of a bountiful harvest tomorrow.

Most investments do not yield an immediate return. That's just a fact of life. You can plant the seed, but you can't make it rain. Those are the times when you must maintain hope for the future. Don't ever allow yourself to get stuck in a negative space. Always look to the light at the end of the tunnel. Focus on the purpose rather than the pain. Accept the obstacles in life for what they are. Temporary setbacks. Nothing more.

Unfortunately for us all, happiness is not a constant state of emotion. Accept it. But don't let that fact effect of minimize your level of optimism. Nothing positive develops out of anxiety. Stop worrying about who you are not and what you don't have. Start to enjoy who you are and that which you do have and have accomplished. If you spend all day looking back in the rearview at your past mistakes and regrets then you'll never get to your past mistakes and regrets, then you'll never get your destination of success. As a matter of fact, you had best always keep your eyes on the road ahead. You might find yourself having an accident in the process if you don't.

This will require a certain degree of "memory loss." You

must let go of any negative memories and emotions that you might be holding on to. Since you can't re-live an experience or a moment, simply make room for the new ones to come in. If you hold on to old memories, especially the bad ones, then you may never be able to move forward because you'll be stuck right there in the past. And sometimes you don't realize how bad a situation was until you get out of it. Physically and especially mentally. So never determine or interpret your identity, worth, or potential through the lens or the memory of a single event.

Success is not quantity. Success is quality. This means the quality of the experiences in your life, the quality of the people you surround yourself with, the quality of your self-confidence in your abilities, and the quality of the goals and things you seek to acquire. But above all else, success is in your heart. The meaning of which can be defined by no one else but you … So, in the end, remember, success is when "you" win. ABXXXXLUTELY!!!!!!

# V.I.P RESOURCES

Banks that will approve your new LLC for 50k no documents or income required:

- Lendino
- Blue Vine
- Business loans.com
- Backed
- On Deck
- National Business Capital
- Credibly
- Kickplay

# V.I.P RESOURCES

## AI TOOLS

- SEO—Usestyle.ai
- Voice—Lovo.ai
- Excel—Numerous.ai
- Chatbot—Dante.ai
- Videos—Pixverse.ai
- Content—Popai.pro
- Website—10Web.io
- Slides—Decktopus.com
- Images—Rendernet.ai
- Automation—Questflow.ai

# V.I.P RESOURCES

10 business credit cards you can apply for without using your social security number

- Sam's Club
- Capital on Tap
- Hatch
- Divvy
- Clear Bank
- Torpago
- Emburse
- Charity
- Ramp
- Bred

# V.I.P RESOURCES

5 banks soft pulls:

- Penfed Credit Union
- Alliant Credit Union
- Digital Federal Credit Union
- First Tech Federal Credit Union
- Consumers Credit Union

# V.I.P RESOURCES

5 Best Business Loans for Bad Credit (24 To 72 hour Funding)

1. Credibly.com
   Minimum 500 + 6 months in business
2. Fora Financial
   Minimum 500 credit score + 6 months in business
3. Quickbridge
   Minimum 600 credit score + 6 months in business
4. Fundbox
   Minimum 600 credit score + 6 months in business
5. Taycor Financial
   Minimum 550 credit score + less than 2 years in business

# V.I.P RESOURCES

Best AI tools to use in 2024

- ViralityAI.net
- ChatGPT—Does ANYTHING
- ChatSonic—ChatGPT alternative
- Midjourney—Generates Photos
- Leonardo AI—Generates Art
- Rendernet—Generates AI Influencers
- Invideo—Generates Videos
- RunwayML—Turns photo into videos
- Beathoven—Generates Music
- Replit—Generates Viral Videos
- OpusClip—Generates Viral Videos
- Slides AI—Generates Presentations
- Upscale.Media—Make any photo sharper
- Veed.io—AI video Editiing
- Flot.ai—ChatGPT in your right click

# V.I.P RESOURCES

50K Personal Loans

Low Income/Bad Credit

- Achieve.com/Personal-loans:
- Prequalify with no hard inquiry 1 to 3 days funding turnaround. Use of funds is completely up to you choose loan terms & set payment dates
- Loan amounts from $5k to $50k.
- 620 minimum FICO score
- Required Documentation:
  - Proof of income
  - Social Security Number
  - Proof of Identity
  - Employment Status

Go to ADP.com

Achieve pulls your Experian FICO 8

# V.I.P RESOURCES

Top 10 Courier & Delivery Apps

1. Spark
2. Instacart
3. Medspeed
4. Favor Delivery
5. Rappi
6. Atlas Courier
7. Reliable Delivery
8. Capital Express
9. Smart Delivery Service
10. Ameritrans

# V.I.P RESOURCES

8 Tradelines That Don't Do A Credit Check

1. Creditstrong.com

2. Meetava.com

3. Trygrain.com

4. www.cred.ai

5. Kickoff.com

6. Boompay.com

7. StellarFi.com

8. Tillful.com

# ABOUT THE AUTHOR

MICHAEL, ALSO KNOWN AS "OFFICIAL LIL MIKE," IS A multifaceted individual with a diverse array of accomplishments that speak to his resilience and unwavering determination. Hailing originally from Virginia, he spent numerous summers in New York under the care of his grandmother. Despite facing adversity at an early age, Michael's indomitable spirit propelled him to transcend his circumstances.

A seasoned Real Estate Mogul and Investor, Michael has not only conquered the challenging world of real estate but has also become a seasoned talent acquisition consultant with a keen eye for identifying potential in others. His prowess in the music industry, coupled with his known name "Official Lil Mike," attests to his insider status and influence in the realm of music.

Michael's journey is marked by resilience, illustrated vividly by his experience growing up. This pivotal moment did not define him; instead, it fueled his determination to rise above challenges. From the Grammy's red carpet to securing multimillion-dollar real estate deals, Michael's journey exemplifies that no environmental state can hinder the realization of one's true potential.

Beyond his professional achievements, Michael is a passionate Criminal Justice advocate, using his platform to champion meaningful change within the system. Michael has been very vocal about his experiences with probation and parole. His life story serves as an inspiration to many who have faced imperfect circumstances, demonstrating that with unwavering determination, one can overcome obstacles and emerge triumphant. Through his various roles and experiences, Michael continues to embody the essence of an individual who defies expectations, proving that true success knows no boundaries.

Beyond his professional achievements, Michael is a passionate Criminal Justice advocate, using his platform to champion meaningful change within the system. His life story serves as an inspiration to many who have faced imperfect circumstances, demonstrating that with unwavering determination, one can overcome obstacles and rise above. Through his various roles and experiences, Michael continues to embody the essence of an individual who defies expectations, proving that true success knows no boundaries. "Absofuckinglutely!!!"

Printed in the United States
by Baker & Taylor Publisher Services